The Science of Magnets

LIVING SCIENCE

Jonathan Bocknek

Gareth Stevens Publishing
MILWAUKEE

For a free color catalog describing Gareth Stevens' list of high-quality books and multimedia programs, call 1-800-542-2595 (USA) or 1-800-461-9120 (Canada). Gareth Stevens Publishing's Fax: (414) 225-0377.

Library of Congress Cataloging-in-Publication Data available upon request from publisher. Fax (414) 225-0377 for the attention of the Publishing Records Department.

ISBN 0-8368-2572-1 (lib. bdg.)

This edition first published in 2000 by
Gareth Stevens Publishing
1555 North RiverCenter Drive, Suite 201
Milwaukee, WI 53212 USA

Project Co-ordinator: Meaghan Craven
Series Editor: Linda Weigl
Copy Editors: Marg Cook and Rennay Craats
Design and Illustration: Warren Clark and Chantelle Sales
Cover Design: Carole Knox
Layout: Lucinda Cage
Gareth Stevens Editor: Rita Reitci

Printed in Canada

1 2 3 4 5 6 7 8 9 04 03 02 01 00

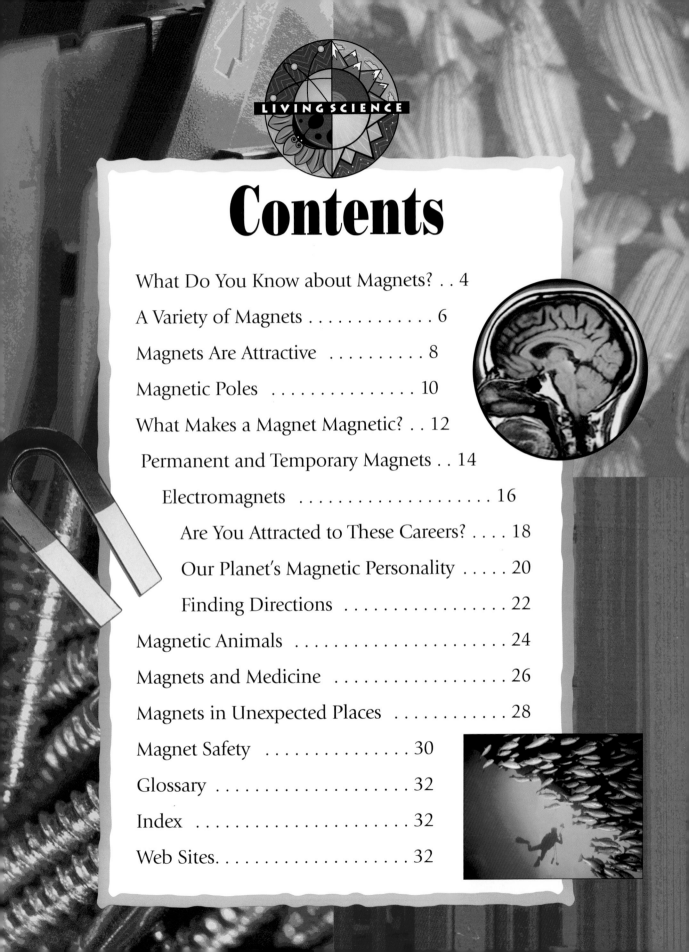

Contents

What Do You Know about Magnets? . . 4

A Variety of Magnets 6

Magnets Are Attractive 8

Magnetic Poles 10

What Makes a Magnet Magnetic? . . 12

Permanent and Temporary Magnets . . 14

Electromagnets 16

Are You Attracted to These Careers? 18

Our Planet's Magnetic Personality 20

Finding Directions 22

Magnetic Animals 24

Magnets and Medicine 26

Magnets in Unexpected Places 28

Magnet Safety 30

Glossary 32

Index 32

Web Sites. 32

What Do You Know about Magnets?

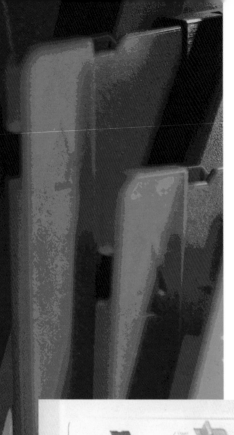

Magnets are all around us. They are a part of almost everything we do. We use magnets every time we:
- listen to the radio
- ring a doorbell
- talk on the telephone
- use a can opener
- watch television

Some can openers have small magnets that hold onto can lids.

Magnets are hidden inside radios.

There are magnets almost everywhere in our homes. Peek inside the kitchen cupboards. They may have magnets holding them shut. Many home appliances have magnets, too. There are magnets inside electric fans and hair dryers.

Most magnets are hidden. We do not even know they are there.

Computers and telephones have magnets inside.

A Variety of Magnets

Many magnets are human-made. We make magnets by mixing the **magnetic** metals iron, nickel, or cobalt with other materials. Then we form the magnets into different shapes.

Magnets come in many shapes, sizes, and strengths. We often name magnets by their shape.

Type

Bar Magnet	Rod Magnet	Horseshoe Magnet

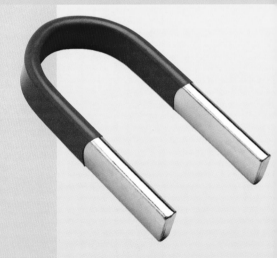

| rectangular, flat | round, long | U-shaped |

Example of Use

Lifts heavy metal objects, such as lost boat motors from the bottom of lakes	Used in a tool to pick up dropped screws and bolts	Once used inside some small electric motors and electric doorbells

Other magnets occur naturally. If you dip a magnet into a sand pile, it attracts dark-colored sand grains. These sand grains are tiny bits of a rock called **magnetite**. Magnetite is a natural magnet found in the ground.

Puzzler

Magnets are often named by their shape. There are horseshoe magnets, ring magnets, disk magnets, and rod magnets.

If you could rename them, what would you call these magnets?

Answer: Here are two possibilities. A ring magnet could be called a donut magnet. A disk magnet could be called a pancake magnet.

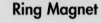

Disk Magnet	Ring Magnet

round, flat	round, flat, hole in center
Holds keyrings to refrigerator doors Used in magnetic earrings	Used in speakers

Magnets Are Attractive

Magnets **attract** most materials that contain the metals iron, nickel, or cobalt. Magnets themselves are made from these metals. This means that magnets attract each other, too.

Magnets are attracted to refrigerator doors that contain iron.

Iron is a metal that can be found in rocks like this one.

Some things that might seem to attract magnets do not. A magnet will not attract an object if it contains only a small amount of iron, nickel, or cobalt. The U.S. nickel coin has too much copper to attract a magnet. The **atoms** of **hematite**, an iron mineral, are arranged in a way that keeps it from attracting magnets.

A magnet will not attract a U.S. five-cent coin. Even though it is called a nickel, it is made mostly of copper.

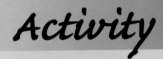

Activity

Pick It Up!

Using a magnet, try picking up the following items.

1. Keys
2. A paper clip
3. A spoon

Try picking up some other items that you think might be attracted to magnets. Which items pick up? Why? Which do not? Why not?

We use the iron in hematite for many things. The color red ocher, often used in paints and dyes, has iron from hematite in it.

Magnetic Poles

Every magnet has two **magnetic poles**. These are the spots where the magnetic effect is strongest. The poles are at opposite ends of the magnet. One is called the north pole. The other is called the south pole.

The letter N or the color red marks a magnet's north pole. The letter S or the color blue marks the south pole.

Two different poles attract each other. A north pole attracts a south pole and a south pole attracts a north pole. A scientist would say that unlike poles attract.

When two poles of the same kind come together, they do not attract. Instead, they **repel**, or push away from each other. For example, two north poles repel each other. A scientist would say that like poles repel.

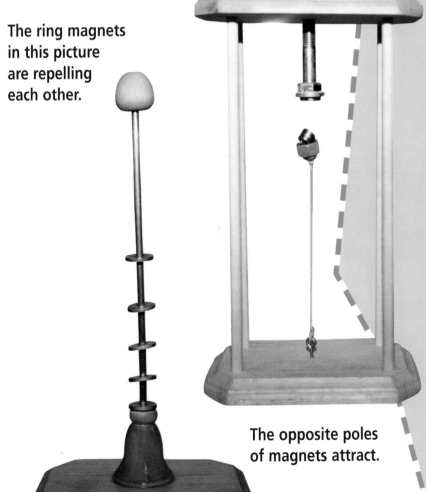

The ring magnets in this picture are repelling each other.

The opposite poles of magnets attract.

Invisible Touch

You will need two small disk magnets and two squares of cardboard.

1. Tape one magnet to the center of each cardboard square. The magnets should have like poles pointing up.
2. Place one square on the table, magnet side up.
3. Hold the other square in your hand. The magnet should point away from your hand.
4. Slowly bring the magnet in your hand close to the magnet on the table. Can you make the magnet on the table move without touching it?

What Makes a Magnet Magnetic?

Scientists picture a magnet as having many tiny magnets inside. These tiny magnets line up. All their north poles point one way. This gives the magnet its north pole. All their south poles point the other way. This gives the magnet its south pole. If any of these tiny magnets do not line up, the magnet loses some of its strength.

North pole   South pole

Magnets are strongest when the tiny magnetic parts in them line up perfectly.

The size of a magnet does not always show its strength. Some very small magnets are stronger than magnets one hundred times bigger. A magnet's strength depends on the materials from which it is made and how well the tiny magnets inside it line up.

Stars called magnetars are the biggest, strongest magnets in the universe.

Permanent and Temporary Magnets

Permanent magnets keep their magnetic strength for a long time. The rock magnetite is a permanent magnet. The magnets that stick to refrigerator doors are permanent magnets, too.

A temporary magnet keeps its magnetic strength for only a short time. If a piece of iron touches a magnet, the tiny magnets inside the iron line up. The iron becomes a temporary magnet.

The screws touching this magnet attract one another. They have become temporary magnets.

Permanent magnets may become weak. The tiny magnets inside permanent magnets are lined up strongly. This changes if a magnet is dropped often or heated for a long time. The tiny magnets begin to point in different directions. The permanent magnet soon becomes very weak.

Heat can damage a permanent magnet.

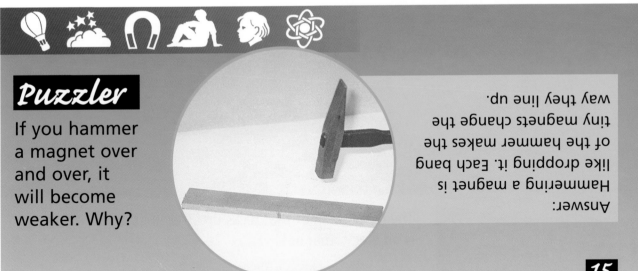

Puzzler

If you hammer a magnet over and over, it will become weaker. Why?

Answer: Hammering a magnet is like dropping it. Each bang of the hammer makes the tiny magnets change the way they line up.

Electromagnets

Electricity produces a **magnetic field** around the wire through which it flows. The more electricity flowing through the wire, the stronger the magnetic field. This effect is called **electromagnetism**. We use electromagnetism to create electromagnets. Electromagnets work like natural magnets. They attract items that contain iron, nickel, or cobalt.

The large magnet that picks up scrap metal is an electromagnet.

An electric motor has two electromagnets inside. One cannot move; the other can. Their magnetic fields push and pull on the one that can move, making it spin. This is how the motor works.

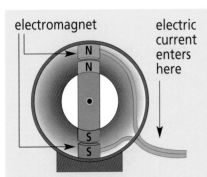

1. An electromagnet is attached to the part of the motor that does not move.

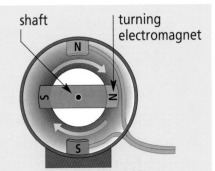

2. Another magnet is attached to the part that moves – the shaft.

3. The non-moving magnet's north pole pulls on the moving magnet's south pole. The shaft turns.

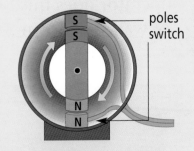

4. The electric current changes direction. The poles of the magnets switch places.

5. The same poles of the magnets touch and repel. The shaft turns.

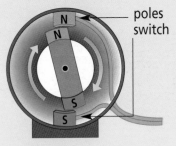

6. The current keeps switching, so the shaft keeps turning.

Puzzler

Is an electromagnet a permanent magnet or a temporary magnet?

Answer: An electromagnet can be very strong, like a permanent magnet. However, it is a temporary magnet. Its magnetic effects last only while electricity is supplied to it.

Are You Attracted to These Careers?

Would you like to be an electrical operator? An electrical operator works with giant magnets that supply homes with electricity. The magnets are in power stations at **dams**. Falling water makes the magnets spin inside huge metal coils. This creates electricity.

An electrical operator controls how much electricity the spinning magnets create. The operator does this by adjusting the amount of water that comes into the power station.

Electrical operators control large amounts of water.

Other careers that involve magnets include geology and telephone repair. Geology is the study of rocks.

A telephone repair person works with magnets inside telephones. Climbing tall telephone poles is also part of the job!

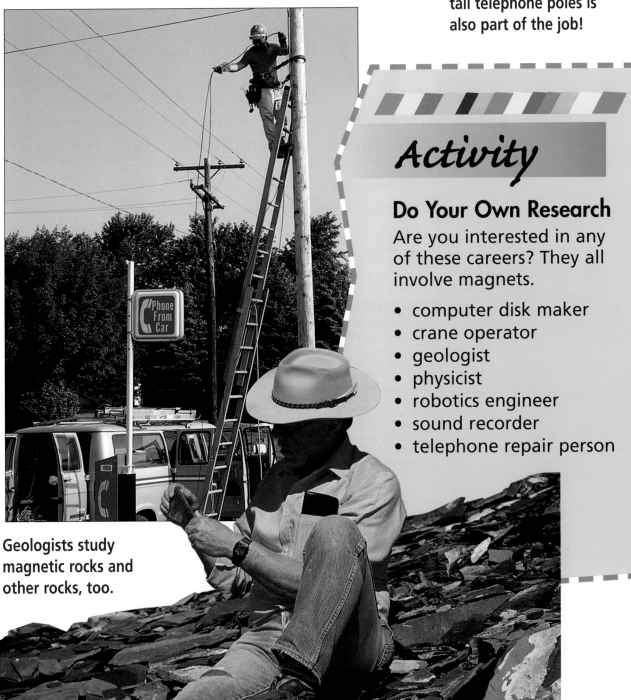

Geologists study magnetic rocks and other rocks, too.

Activity

Do Your Own Research
Are you interested in any of these careers? They all involve magnets.

- computer disk maker
- crane operator
- geologist
- physicist
- robotics engineer
- sound recorder
- telephone repair person

Our Planet's Magnetic Personality

We live on a giant magnet! Our planet acts as if it has a huge bar magnet inside. Earth has a north magnetic pole and a south magnetic pole. It also has an invisible magnetic field all around it.

Earth's magnetic field is called the **magnetosphere**. The magnetosphere is very large. It reaches far into space. It is strongest at the north and south magnetic poles.

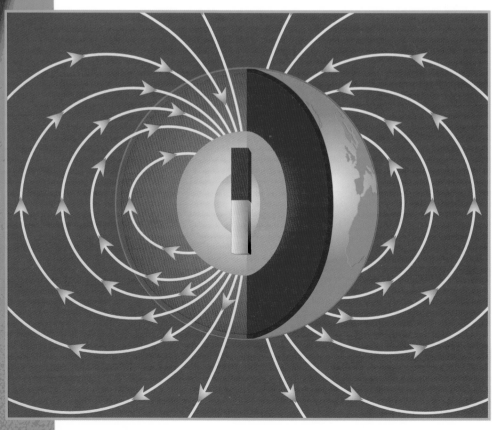

Earth's magnetic field is invisible, but very strong.

When people talk about the north and south poles, they are usually talking about **geographic poles**. Earth's geographic poles are not the same as its magnetic poles. They are in different places. The magnetic north pole is in Canada, about 1,000 miles (1,600 kilometers) away from the geographic north pole. The magnetic south pole is off the coast of Antarctica, south of Melborne, Australia. The geographic south pole lies near the center of Antarctica.

Particles from the Sun often become trapped in Earth's magnetic field at the poles. These particles glow when they strike other particles in Earth's atmosphere. We call these glowing particles the northern and southern lights.

Puzzler

If you want to watch the northern lights at night, where is the best place to be?
- Mexico City, Mexico
- Paris, France
- Los Angeles, USA
- Churchill, Canada

Answer:
Churchill is closest to the north magnetic pole. People who live in Churchill can see the northern lights many nights of the year.

Finding Directions

If a bar magnet hangs from a string, one pole of the magnet always points north. This is called the magnet's north-seeking pole. It is attracted to Earth's north magnetic pole.

About one thousand years ago, people learned to magnetize a needle with a piece of magnetite. They set it so that it could swing freely to point north. Ships used this to find their way.

During the day, ships found north by using a magnetized needle. At night, stars showed their direction.

The sailors had the right idea. A magnet that is free to swing around is called a compass. A compass looks like a round clock. Instead of numbers, the compass face shows the letters N, E, S, and W. They stand for north, east, south, and west. We use a compass to find our directions.

Activity

Make a Compass
Ask an adult to help you with this activity.

1. Stroke a small sewing needle with a magnet. This will turn it into a temporary magnet. Watch out for the sharp point.
2. Push the needle through something that floats. A piece of cork works well.
3. Fill a bucket or a large pan with water. Float your magnet in the middle.

You have just made a compass! Put it in different places around your home. Does it always tell you where north is?

The compasses on ships and airplanes are bar magnets that float in a liquid.

Magnetic Animals

Each autumn, many animals **migrate** to warmer parts of the world. For example, monarch butterflies fly from Canada and the northern United States to places in California and Mexico. Birds and whales travel much farther. How do they find their way over such great distances?

The animals have tiny bits of magnetite in their brains. These small magnets work like compasses. They help the animals stay on course over long distances.

The magnetite in a right whale's body helps the whale find its way from the cold waters of the Arctic to warmer waters and feeding grounds.

Most animals have magnetite in their bodies. This includes you and other people, too. Some kinds of **bacteria** also have magnetite in them.

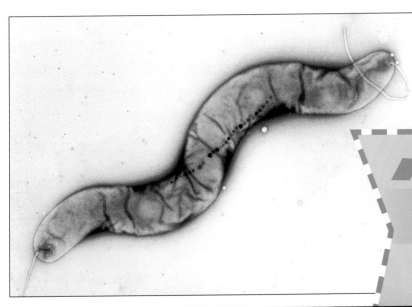

The black dots in the center of this bacterium are tiny pieces of magnetite.

Activity

Make a List

What other animals can you think of that migrate? Make a list of these animals and check your list by looking up each animal in an encyclopedia.

Your list might include animals such as geese, salmon, and tortoises.

Humans and fish have magnetite in their bodies.

Magnets and Medicine

D octors sometimes use electromagnets to discover what is making a person sick. The electromagnets are in a machine called an **MRI**. These letters stand for magnetic resonance imaging. The MRI takes pictures that show the inside of a person's body.

An MRI helps doctors see human body parts, such as the brain.

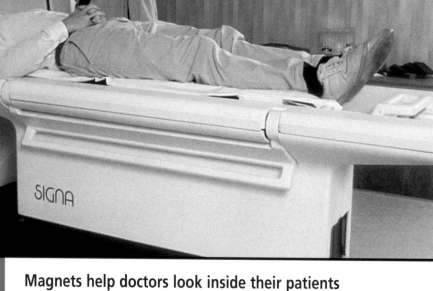

Magnets help doctors look inside their patients without operating.

Another machine used by doctors has giant electromagnets inside. Doctors use the machine to treat a disease called cancer. The electromagnets speed up tiny particles until they are moving very fast. Then the machine shoots the particles at the cancer. The particles destroy the cancer without harming the rest of the patient's body.

Machines with electromagnets inside treat eye cancer.

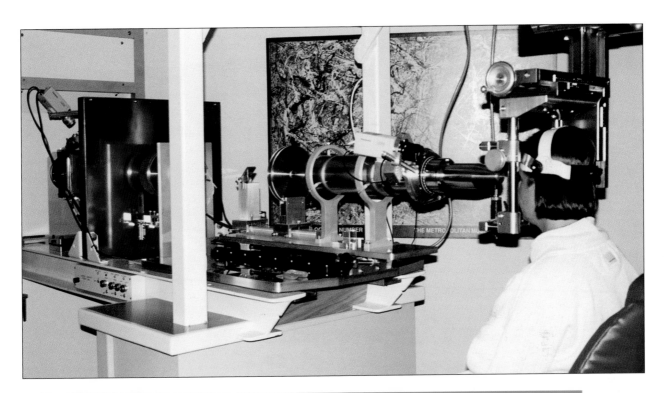

Puzzler

Can magnets hurt people?

Answer:
Magnets are usually safe, but it is important to handle them with care. Do not let strong magnets snap together suddenly. They can pinch fingers caught between them. The magnets might also chip. The chips can do harm if they fly into your eyes.

Magnets in Unexpected Places

Magnets turn up in some unexpected places. Which of these places do you already know about? Do you know of any others?

Security Gates
at airports keep people from taking weapons on the plane. Electromagnets in the doorway detect weapons if people try to sneak them through.

Metal Goal Posts
are held down by magnets just under the surface of the ice. The goal posts come away easily if a hockey player falls into them. The player is not hurt.

Credit Cards

store information about the person who owns them.
The thin, black bar on the back is coated in tiny magnets. The patterns they make hold the information.

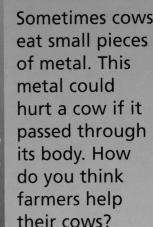

Audio Tapes and Video Tapes

are coated with millions of tiny magnets.
An electromagnet makes the tiny magnets line up in different patterns. These patterns record sounds and pictures.

Checks and Paper Money

are printed with magnetic ink.
This helps banks and police tell if someone is using fake money or checks.

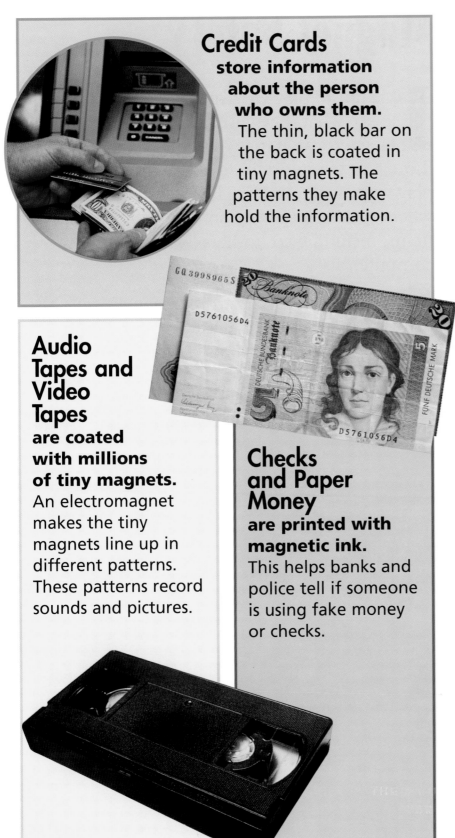

Puzzler

Sometimes cows eat small pieces of metal. This metal could hurt a cow if it passed through its body. How do you think farmers help their cows?

Answer:
Some farmers give their cows small magnets to swallow. They are called cow magnets. Cows have four stomachs. The cow magnet stays in the cow's first or second stomach. It has rounded ends, so it does not hurt the cow. Any metal the cow eats sticks to the cow magnet.

Magnet Safety

It is fun to play with magnets. It is exciting to see what they will attract or repel. Magnets can damage certain objects, though. It is important to be careful where you play with magnets. It is also up to you to know where your magnets are so they will not damage items, including computers, watches, and computer disks.

People who work with strong magnets must also be careful. Strong magnets at car factories, for example, can damage tools. This sign was posted at a factory — "Beware: Big Magnet Eats Tools."

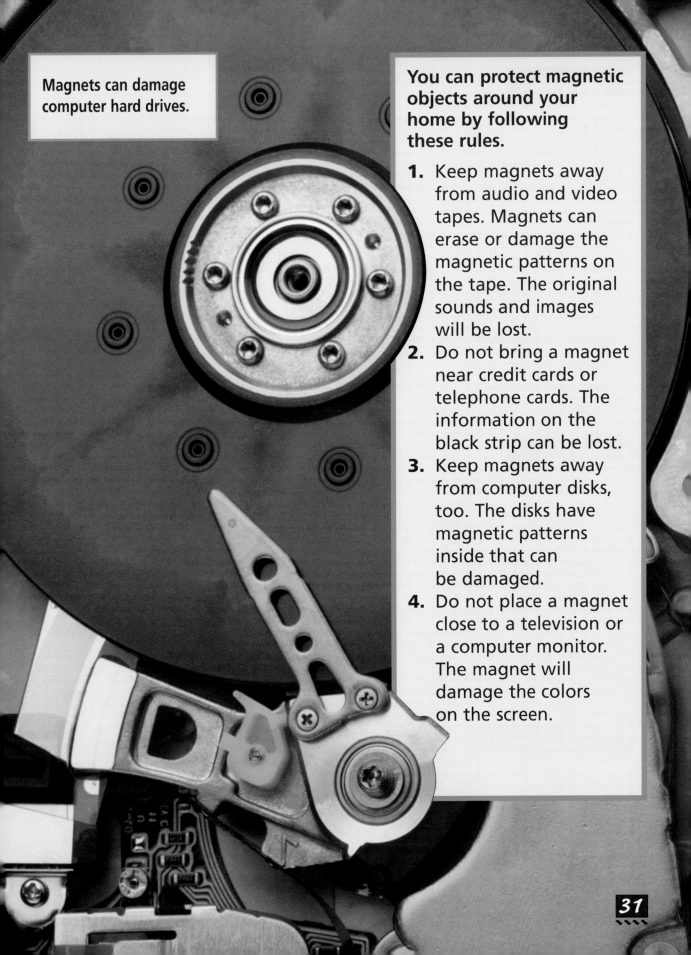

Magnets can damage computer hard drives.

You can protect magnetic objects around your home by following these rules.

1. Keep magnets away from audio and video tapes. Magnets can erase or damage the magnetic patterns on the tape. The original sounds and images will be lost.
2. Do not bring a magnet near credit cards or telephone cards. The information on the black strip can be lost.
3. Keep magnets away from computer disks, too. The disks have magnetic patterns inside that can be damaged.
4. Do not place a magnet close to a television or a computer monitor. The magnet will damage the colors on the screen.

Glossary

atmosphere: the layers of gases that surround and protect Earth.

atoms: tiny particles that make up all matter in the universe.

attract: to pull toward.

bacteria: some of the tiniest living things; each has just a single cell.

collage: a collection and display of different objects or materials.

dam: a wall built to hold back flowing water.

electromagnetism: magnetism produced by current electricity.

geographic poles: the places farthest north and farthest south on Earth; the north and south poles.

hematite: a mineral that supplies most of the world's iron.

magnetic: acting like a magnet.

magnetic field: invisible area where a magnet has power to affect magnetic objects.

magnetic poles: the ends of a magnet, where the magnetic effects are the strongest.

magnetite: a type of iron stone that is very magnetic.

magnetosphere: the magnetic field surrounding Earth.

migrate: travel to a different place when the season changes.

motor: a machine that changes electrical energy into movement.

MRI: a machine that helps people see inside the human body.

repel: to push away.

Index

attract 8, 9, 11, 16, 18, 22
audio tape 29, 31

bacteria 25
bar magnet 6, 20, 22, 23

cancer 27
cobalt 6, 8, 9, 16
compass 23, 24
credit cards 29, 31

disk magnet 7, 11

Earth 20, 21, 22
electrical operator 18
electromagnet 16, 17, 26, 27, 28, 29
electromagnetism 16

geographic north pole 21
geographic south pole 21
geologist 19

hematite 9
hockey 28

horseshoe magnet 6, 7

iron 6, 8, 9, 14, 16

magnetic field 16, 17, 20
magnetic north pole 20, 21, 22
magnetic south pole 20, 21
magnetite 7, 14, 22, 24, 25
magnetosphere 20

motor 6, 17
MRI 26

nickel 6, 8, 9, 16

permanent magnet 14, 15, 17

ring magnet 7, 11

temporary magnet 14, 17, 23

Web Sites

www.kids-spot.com/magnets.htm

ww.surfnetkids.com/electric.htm

aoss.engin.umich.edu/earth_space/magnets8.html

castle.uvic.ca/educ/lfrancis/web/A-WEBPAGE.html

Some web sites stay current longer than others. For further web sites, use your search engines to locate the following topics: *aurora, compass, magnetic fields,* and *rare earth magnets.*